LIFE IN THE MILITARY

LIFE IN THE
US SPECIAL OPERATIONS FORCES

by Laura Platas Scott

BrightPoint Press

San Diego, CA

BrightPoint Press

© 2021 BrightPoint Press
an imprint of ReferencePoint Press, Inc.
Printed in the United States

For more information, contact:
BrightPoint Press
PO Box 27779
San Diego, CA 92198
www.BrightPointPress.com

ALL RIGHTS RESERVED.

No part of this work covered by the copyright hereon may be reproduced or used in any form or by any means—graphic, electronic, or mechanical, including photocopying, recording, taping, web distribution, or information storage retrieval systems—without the written permission of the publisher.

LIBRARY OF CONGRESS CATALOGING-IN-PUBLICATION DATA

Names: Scott, Laura Platas, 1959 - author.
Title: Life in the US Special Operations Forces / by Laura Platas Scott.
Description: San Diego, CA : ReferencePoint Press, [2021] | Series: Life in the military | Includes index and bibliographic references. | Audience: Grades 10-12
Identifiers: LCCN 2020002418 (print) | LCCN 2020002419 (eBook) | ISBN 9781682829790 (hardcover) | ISBN 9781682829806 (eBook)
Subjects: LCSH: Special forces (Military science)--United States. | Special operations (Military science)--United States.
Classification: LCC U262 .P59 2021 (print) | LCC U262 (eBook) | DDC 356/.16--dc23
LC record available at https://lccn.loc.gov/2020002418
LC eBook record available at https://lccn.loc.gov/2020002419

CONTENTS

AT A GLANCE	4
INTRODUCTION A SPECIAL MISSION	6
CHAPTER ONE HOW DO PEOPLE JOIN THE SPECIAL OPERATIONS FORCES?	14
CHAPTER TWO WHAT TYPES OF JOBS ARE AVAILABLE?	30
CHAPTER THREE WHAT IS DAILY LIFE LIKE?	48
CHAPTER FOUR WHAT IS DEPLOYMENT LIKE?	62
Glossary	74
Source Notes	75
For Further Research	76
Index	78
Image Credits	79
About the Author	80

AT A GLANCE

- US special operations forces (SOFs) are made up of elite troops that take on some of the toughest, riskiest, and most important military missions.

- Each branch of the military has its own SOFs.

- People who want to join the SOFs usually must be in the military already. They must then go through additional training and testing to join one of these forces.

- In 2020 there were about 70,000 people in the US military's SOFs.

- Members of the SOFs have many different jobs. Their main mission is usually fighting. But they may also be doctors, engineers, communications experts, dog trainers, and even veterinarians.

- Being in the SOFs often requires special skills. Members of the SOFs may have to climb mountains, parachute from airplanes, dive underwater, and do many other things.

- Members of the SOFs need to use a lot of different gear. They may use night vision headgear, a variety of weapons, special vehicles, and other tools.

- Special forces troops deploy to many different countries. They may work alongside another nation's military. Their missions are often secret.

- Besides fighting, special forces also help with disaster relief missions around the world.

INTRODUCTION

A SPECIAL MISSION

It was the middle of the night on October 26, 2019. Eight helicopters flew to a small town in Syria. The town was near the border with Turkey. Inside the helicopters were about seventy soldiers. Their mission was top secret. The soldiers were a US Army special operations force (SOF). They were part of a group called

Special operations forces use helicopters on many of their missions.

Delta Force. Their job was to find Abu Bakr al-Baghdadi. This man was known as the world's most dangerous **terrorist**.

The US military had been hunting al-Baghdadi for about ten years. He had stayed hidden. He moved often. He trusted no one. But Delta Force had found his hiding place. It was a house with a wall around it.

The soldiers blew a hole in the wall. Al-Baghdadi's men fired at the soldiers. The soldiers killed some of these men. They took two men as prisoners.

Delta Force brought a dog to help find al-Baghdadi. There were tunnels underneath the house. Al-Baghdadi ran to these tunnels. The soldiers and the dog

Military working dogs are helpful companions on tough missions.

Aircraft flying overhead sometimes support special operations forces on the ground.

chased him. They soon found him. He was in a room in the tunnel. He ran to a smaller tunnel. He was trapped. He could not escape.

Al-Baghdadi wore a vest with explosives. He died when he set off the vest. None of the soldiers were killed. The dog was injured but recovered.

Delta Force searched the building for two hours. They gathered information. Then they left. US warplanes bombed the hiding place. The building was destroyed. The soldiers had succeeded in their mission.

WHO ARE THE SPECIAL OPERATIONS FORCES?

SOFs carry out challenging missions. Delta Force is just one of these forces. The branches of the military have their

Special Operations Forces by Military Branch

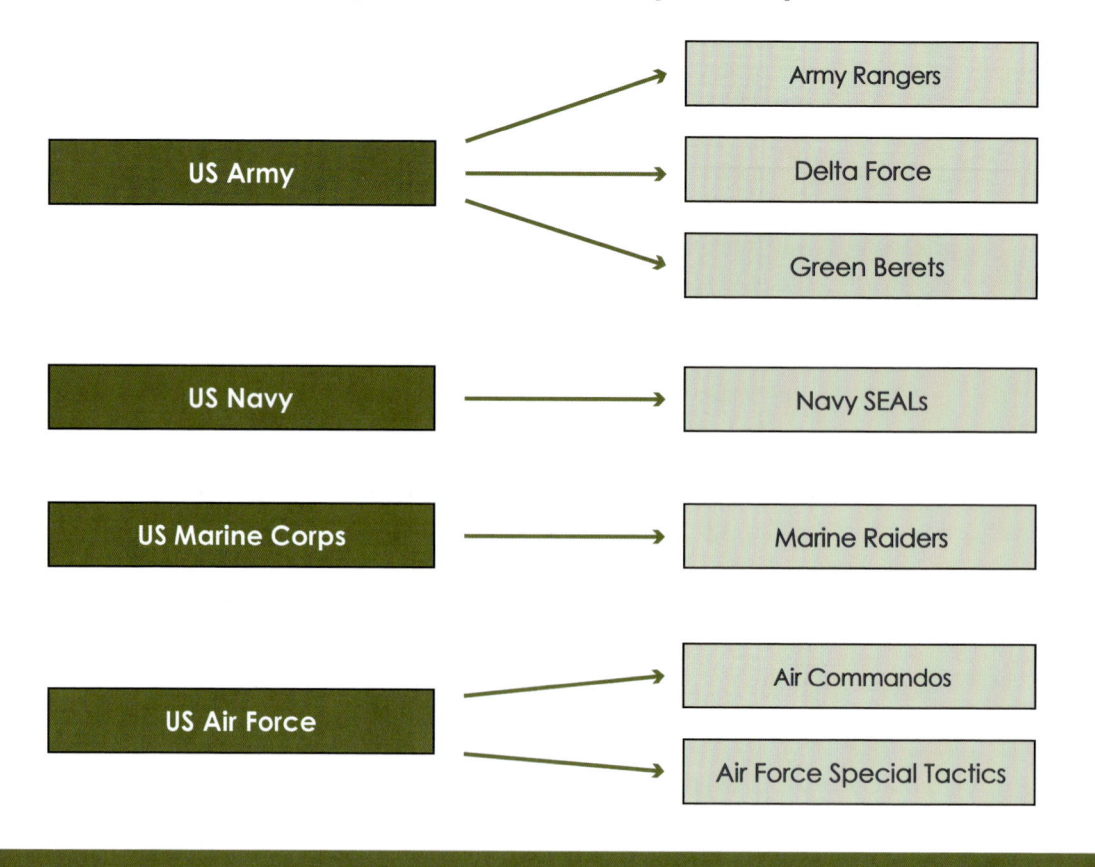

US Army	Army Rangers, Delta Force, Green Berets
US Navy	Navy SEALs
US Marine Corps	Marine Raiders
US Air Force	Air Commandos, Air Force Special Tactics

The US military's special operations forces are divided among the military's branches. These are some of the major SOFs.

own special forces. The US Army has the Army Rangers, the Green Berets, and Delta Force. The US Army Rangers is the largest of these. Delta Force is the smallest.

The US Air Force has the Air Commandos. It also has US Air Force Special Tactics. The Marine Raiders is part of the US Marine Corps. The Navy SEALs is another special force. It is part of the US Navy. The word SEAL stands for Sea, Air, and Land. There are several SEAL teams.

CHAPTER ONE

HOW DO PEOPLE JOIN THE SPECIAL OPERATIONS FORCES?

There are many steps people must take to join an SOF. They usually must first join a branch of the military. Joining the military is called enlisting. Each branch of the military has recruiters. They work in

Soldiers talk to high school students about what jobs are in the military. Some of those jobs are in special operations forces.

offices all over the country. Recruiters meet with people. They explain how to enlist.

A person must be a US resident to enlist. She must have a high school diploma or a General Education Diploma. There are age requirements too. Seventeen-year-olds can enlist if a parent gives permission. Eighteen-year-olds do not need permission. The oldest age allowed varies from branch to branch.

THE ENLISTING PROCESS

Recruiters schedule visits to a Military Entrance Processing Station (MEPS). There are dozens of MEPS in the country. People take an exam on their first visit. The exam is called the Armed Services Vocational Aptitude Battery (ASVAB) test. It measures people's abilities in different subjects. It tests math and science knowledge. It also assesses reading and writing skills. An ASVAB score shows a person's strengths. It helps the person see which jobs would be the best fit. Those who do not pass can retake it. But they must wait one month before retaking it. Some people may take the ASVAB test at their high school.

SPECIAL OPERATIONS FORCES BY THE NUMBERS

About 1.38 million people were active duty members of the military in 2020. Of those, about 70,000 people were in the SOFs. There were 33,000 soldiers in the army's special forces. There were 10,000 sailors in the navy's special forces. About 3,000 troops served in the marines' special forces. And there were about 21,000 airmen in the air force's special forces.

In February 2020, an astronaut led recruits in an enlistment ceremony from space.

The next step is a medical exam. A person's height and weight are measured. A doctor checks hearing and vision. There are blood tests. There are also drug tests.

The military wants to make sure recruits are healthy.

Then people meet with a counselor. Counselors help people find the right military job. They look at people's ASVAB scores. The branches have different score requirements. Scores also show what job a person might be best at. The counselors discuss which jobs are a good fit. Jobs in the military are known by a code. This code is called a military occupational specialty (MOS). Each job has its own MOS code.

Next, people must sign the enlistment agreement. This is a **contract**. It explains how long people will serve in the military. An enlistment is usually for four years. People can reenlist to serve more years once this time is up.

BASIC TRAINING

A training period follows enlistment. It is called basic training or boot camp. It lasts eight to twelve weeks. A person in basic training is called a recruit. Recruits learn a daily routine. Much of their training is physical.

Each military branch has physical requirements. Recruits do push-ups and sit-ups. They must run 2 miles (3 km).

Weapons training is an important part of basic training.

The passing scores or times depend on the recruit's age and gender. Navy recruits also have a swimming test.

Recruits also have classroom training. They learn the history of their military branch. They have weapons training too. They learn how to fire and clean a rifle.

Recruits take tests at the end of basic training. Recruits are tested on what they have learned in the classroom. They are tested for physical fitness. And they are

SOF HISTORY

The Green Berets were the first SOF. The US Army formed this group in 1952. The Green Berets helped out with missions that required just a few soldiers. They wore green hats called berets.

The US Navy SEALs were the second SOF. This group was formed in 1962. SEALs were trained to fight on land and in water. They fought in the Vietnam War (1954–1975). They destroyed underwater mines. They also fought the enemy in the jungle.

tested on using weapons. Those who pass graduate from the program.

Recruits who graduate go through a ceremony. They become active duty members of the military. This means they will serve full-time.

JOINING THE SPECIAL OPERATIONS FORCES

People who want to join an SOF usually must be active duty. They must be at least twenty years old. They need a security clearance. This means the government trusts them to keep important information secret. They have to pass another physical fitness test. They do sit-ups and push-ups. They bench press weights. There is a climbing exercise too. People must climb a rope while wearing a heavy vest. They must also run 5 miles (8 km) while wearing a heavy **rucksack**.

Passing the physical fitness test is the first step. Then recruits go through a training period. The length of this training depends on the force. Training can take more than a year. Recruits train every day. They run and swim. They climb ropes. They practice parachuting from airplanes. They learn how to read maps. They also learn survival skills

Recruits are challenged physically and mentally by tough obstacle courses.

so they can find food and water. Recruits have more weapons training too.

The final step is a field test. It is a fake mission. It can take up to two weeks

The tough and realistic Robin Sage field test prepares Green Berets for real missions.

to complete. There are different field tests. For example, the field test for Green Berets recruits is called Robin Sage. Recruits parachute into a pretend country called Pineland. It is spread across twenty-one counties in North Carolina. Recruits must free Pineland. They use all their training to fight a pretend war. Their guns are not loaded with real bullets. But the field test is very realistic. Army officials tell residents about the exercise beforehand. They say, "Residents may hear blank gunfire and see occasional flares. Controls are in place to ensure there is no risk to persons or property."[1]

Delta Force often selects troops who are already in an SOF. They may recruit from the US Army Rangers. They may also recruit from the US Navy SEALs.

Sometimes they choose people from the Coast Guard.

SOF members must be brave. They must never give up. Quitting is not an option. Teamwork is the most important part of any mission.

> **THE TOUGHEST MAN ALIVE**
>
> David Goggins is a former navy officer. He lost 100 pounds (45 kg) in three months to join the navy. He later completed SEAL training. He also graduated from the Army Ranger School. He completed air force special forces training too. He is the only person to have completed all three. Some people call him the toughest man alive. Goggins says, "The harder something is the more it was challenging my mind."
>
> *Quoted in "Maybe the Toughest Man Alive," Department of Defense, December 7, 2018. www.defense.gov.*

On March 29, 2019, Acting Secretary of Defense Patrick Shanahan attended a ceremony at the US Special Operations Command in Tampa, Florida. This command oversees all of the nation's SOFs. He told the special operations forces that they receive "admiration from your fellow citizens, comfort from our allies and partners and fear from our adversaries."[2]

CHAPTER TWO

WHAT TYPES OF JOBS ARE AVAILABLE?

In an SOF, people work in teams. Everyone on a team has a special job. The stakes are high. A team member could die if someone does not do his or her job right. The members of the SOF need to trust each other. Their training gives them the confidence to succeed.

Green Berets train aboard a helicopter in Kentucky.

ARMY SPECIAL FORCES

Many people who work in the SOFs have combat jobs. They play an important role in defending the country.

Soldiers in the Green Berets serve in combat teams. These teams are called Operational Detachment Alphas (ODAs). There are usually twelve soldiers in each ODA. Two of the soldiers are weapons sergeants. They know how to use many types of weapons. Some weapons are used against enemy soldiers. Others are used against enemy vehicles. Weapons sergeants go behind enemy lines. They may disconnect mines.

Two other soldiers on an ODA are communications sergeants. They help team members talk to each other on missions.

Weapons sergeants train to use not only US weapons, but also the weapons of foreign militaries.

Another two are medical sergeants. There are also two engineering sergeants. These soldiers build or destroy structures. The operations sergeant organizes missions.

The intelligence sergeant studies the enemy. Commanders lead the group. There is a commander and an assistant commander.

AIR FORCE SPECIAL OPERATIONS

The members of US Air Force SOFs can have several jobs. Some are special tactics operators. They plan air missions. They tell pilots what to do during a mission. Pilots support ground combat troops. For example, an operator might order an aircraft to bomb enemy territory. This type of action helps SOFs on the ground.

Michael West was a chief master sergeant. He served in Afghanistan in

Air Commandos train in hand-to-hand fighting.

2006. He worked as a special tactics combat controller. In this job, he helped military aircraft work with special forces on the ground. At the time, US SOFs fought the Taliban. The Taliban is a military organization. It supports terrorists. Canadian ground forces helped the US military fight the Taliban. During a mission, West ordered aircraft to bomb the enemy. This action helped save fifty-one US troops. It also saved thirty-three troops from other nations.

In 2017, West was awarded a medal for his service. Lieutenant General Brad Webb gave West this medal. He said, "We knew we could sleep when Mike was working. There is no higher praise in special operations."[3]

The air force special operations also include Air Force Special Reconnaissance (SR). These troops work with other SOF units. They gather information about the weather. They use this information to predict weather conditions in the future. SRs need to know what the weather will

DRONES

SOFs use drones to help with some missions. Drones are a special type of aircraft. They do not have pilots. Troops use remote controls to operate the drones. The drones have cameras. They can find and take photos of enemy forces. Navy SEALs carry drones on ships. These drones can fly over enemy ships. They take photos of the enemy.

Navy SEALs train to parachute from airplanes. This can help them sneak quietly behind enemy lines.

be like before a mission. Bad weather can cause a mission to fail. SRs must practice their parachuting skills. They may have to parachute into enemy areas.

NAVY SEALS AND MARINE RAIDERS

Navy SEALs often sneak up on enemies on beaches or coastlines. They may drop into the sea from a helicopter. Each Navy SEAL swims with a heavy rucksack. Navy SEALs also carry their weapons while they swim. They might have to swim against a current. The seas may be rough. Navy SEALs have to be strong swimmers.

Navy SEALs have many duties. They must be able to operate small boats for water missions. They need to be experts in land warfare too. They must know how to use a variety of weapons. They dive into the water during combat. They drop from aircraft into the sea. They also parachute into enemy areas.

WORKING WITH DOGS

Dogs sometimes help with SOF missions. Canine handlers train dogs to recognize certain scents. That way, the dogs can search for a person or an object. They can find explosives. Handlers and their dogs also train together. For example, they practice swimming long distances together.

One role in the Marine Raiders is Special Operations Capabilities Specialist. These marines have different specialties. Some of them help marines communicate. Others work with intelligence troops. Some are canine handlers. Canine handlers train and work with dogs. Trained dogs can help with missions.

Another Marine Raider job is Combat Service Support. These troops drive special vehicles. They are tough warriors.

THE GREEN BERETS

Members of the SOFs use special tools that help them do their jobs. The Green Berets

Night vision goggles give special operations forces an advantage over enemies in the dark.

use Ground Mobility Vehicles in missions. These are lightweight vehicles. They can move over rocky land. They can also drive through mud.

Green Berets jump out of airplanes. They wear special helmets. The air gets thinner the higher up soldiers go. They need more oxygen. These helmets supply them with oxygen. Green Berets also use special parachutes. The parachutes can still work in severe weather.

Green Berets do their missions at night. They need to be able to see in the dark. They use night vision headgear. It allows them to see at night. It also works in dark caves and in smoky areas.

Sometimes Green Berets need to go through water. They use a device called a rebreather. It helps them breathe underwater.

SUPPORT AND NON-COMBAT JOBS

Some people in the SOFs have support jobs. They help keep their SOF running. One type of support job is an aviation mechanic. Aviation mechanics maintain and repair aircraft.

There are many other types of SOF support jobs. Doctors keep troops healthy.

Keeping helicopters working properly is important for the SOFs.

They also help people in other countries. They give people **vaccines**. They give refugees medical care. Refugees are people who flee their home countries to escape danger.

Special operations teams train for emergency medical responses.

Another noncombat job is veterinarian. Troops may go on a mission in a farming area. Enemy fighters may hide among innocent villagers. If special forces veterinarians can help treat farm animals, they can build trust with the people. This trust can help them accomplish missions. Combat is an important part of the SOFs. But these **elite** forces do more than fight enemies. Many types of experts are needed to carry out their missions.

CHAPTER THREE

WHAT IS DAILY LIFE LIKE?

People in the SOFs train every day. This training prepares them for real missions. They must exercise regularly. They must also practice the special skills needed for their jobs. For example, Navy SEALs practice parachuting. They also go scuba diving. They practice shooting from moving vehicles such as boats.

Underwater missions make diving training important for special operations forces.

Some SOFs hold competitions. Troops participate in these competitions to test their skills. The Marine Corps holds the Marine

Raider Competition each year. Six teams compete in this event. Each team has six Marine Raiders. The troops have to navigate on land. The teams compete in fitness tests too. They have to do a 15-mile (24-km) march. Each person carries a rucksack. The rucksack weighs at least 45 pounds

TEAM BUILDING

SOF troops depend on each other. They must work as a team. They practice teamwork during training. They may have to carry a small boat around. Team members may have to switch hands to get a better grip. They trade places with a person on the opposite side. Working as a team is the only way to succeed.

(20 kg). The troops also practice sliding down ropes. These are the same skills they might need in actual missions.

FURTHER TRAINING

Some SOF troops go through more schooling. This additional training helps them learn new skills. Navy SEAL teams train for breaching. The word *breach* means to go through something. SEALs might face obstacles in their missions. For example, they might have to get past a locked door. In breacher school, they learn to use explosives. They use explosives to knock down doors.

Breaching allows troops to enter locked buildings to find enemies.

Air Commandos go through water survival training. This training happens three times each year. The troops jump into water while wearing parachute gear. They practice releasing their parachutes. This is important so they do not get tangled in the parachutes. Then they practice getting into life rafts.

Members of the SOFs can apply for advanced training. Some missions may involve going underwater. Troops can take a special class to become divers. The class is called the Combat Diver Qualification Course (CDQC). The CDQC is offered at a school in Key West, Florida. The training is physically and mentally challenging.

Special forces members also train in the mountains. During a mission, they may need to hike or drive through rough areas. Or they may need to fly in and parachute from an aircraft. They practice parachuting from different **altitudes**. The planes fly 30,000 feet (9,140 m) or more above the

AIR COMMANDO TRAINING

Troops who are becoming Air Commandos take a special course. It is called the Air Commando Field Skills Course. They train for thirteen days in mock battles. They train to shoot from a moving vehicle. Their training includes three days at a gun range. They practice shooting at targets. This helps them prepare for real missions.

ground. The troops parachute from this height. They have to wear special masks. These masks deliver oxygen.

MISSIONS

Real missions are part of daily life in the SOFs. Troops must always be prepared to leave for a mission. They learn how to plan for a mission. They need to know which equipment to take. They also need to know which weapons to pack. SOF members are involved in many types of missions. They may need to rescue **hostages**. Or they may spy on enemies. Each mission requires expert skills and training.

SOF troops must arrive to areas in secret. They must not be seen or heard. They want to surprise the enemy. SOF teams sometimes arrive in a helicopter. Or they parachute from a plane. They may also arrive by land or sea. In some cases, they arrive on horseback. For example, the Green Berets used horses in a mission in 2001. The mission happened in northern Afghanistan. Twelve Green Berets used horses to sneak up on Taliban soldiers. Captain Mark Nutsch led this team. He grew up on a cattle ranch in Kansas. He never expected to ride a horse in battle.

SOF troops train to use all kinds of transportation—including horses.

He said, "No one had horse saddles ready to go, so we . . . rode the local horses with local saddles and equipment."[4] Nutsch's team was just one of the groups involved. Other SOF teams fought alongside them. Their mission was to remove the Taliban from power. It took them eight weeks to do this.

HOUSING AND EDUCATION

SOF troops live on military bases. A base may be a camp or another type of military property. The military offers housing for troops and their families. They may live in a single-family house or a duplex. A duplex is

Like other kinds of troops, some SOF members live in barracks.

made up of two houses that share a wall. Two families can live in a duplex. Some troops live off base. The military may help pay for the costs of this housing.

Troops who are not married live in barracks. Barracks are buildings that many troops live in together. They share living spaces. Another housing option is apartments. A member of the SOFs can live in an apartment with a roommate.

Military bases are much like normal neighborhoods. There are parks and stores. There are often schools on base. The schools teach troops' children. The schools offer an education for both young children and teenagers.

Troops can take college classes. They might take these classes to get a better

A group of Navy SEALs receive their bachelor's degrees in a 2016 ceremony.

military job. The military helps pay for

this education.

CHAPTER FOUR

WHAT IS DEPLOYMENT LIKE?

Some SOF troops live and work on bases in the United States. Others are **deployed** to other countries. They carry out missions in these countries. An important mission across the world could come up without warning. SOF troops must always be ready for a deployment.

US SOFs were deployed in Afghanistan in 2019.

TYPES OF DEPLOYMENTS

Not all missions involve combat. Some SOF members train troops in other countries. For example, US Army Special Forces

US Air Force SOF members train in cold conditions in Norway in March 2020.

members went to Afghanistan in the 2010s.

They helped train Afghan troops. These

troops were fighting the Islamic State of Iraq

and Syria (ISIS). This terrorist group was causing destruction in Afghanistan.

SOF members may train alongside another country's special forces. For example, Navy SEALs have participated in winter exercises in Norway. Navy SEALs may have missions in cold places. They must train in different environments. In one exercise they parachuted onto frozen lakes. They trained alongside troops from many other countries.

Air Commandos carry out special operations around the world. They have deployed to the Philippines and Africa.

US Army SOFs train alongside their Thai counterparts in a February 2020 exercise.

They help other nations fight terrorism. They also train troops in other countries. They help other militaries with tough missions. Air Commandos also help people recover from natural disasters. They have helped after earthquakes in Haiti and Japan. They traveled to the Philippines after a deadly storm.

FIGHTING TERRORIST FORCES

Many SOFs are deployed around the world to fight terrorism. This mission

FIGHTING IN NIGER

In 2017, a US Army Special Forces team was deployed to Niger. Niger is a country in Africa. The team was there to help Nigerien forces fight terrorism. There are some ISIS fighters in Africa. Another enemy is al-Shabab. This terrorist group is based in East Africa. It has carried out many attacks in the region. The special forces team was ambushed by unknown forces. The enemy shot rocket-propelled grenades at them. The battle lasted hours. Four US troops died.

SOFs have some of the toughest jobs in the military. Their secret missions help keep Americans safe.

became more important to the US military after September 11, 2001. On that day, terrorists hijacked four airplanes in the

United States. One plane hit a military building near Washington, DC. Two others hit skyscrapers in New York City. The fourth crashed into a field in Pennsylvania. Nearly 3,000 people died.

The terrorists involved in these attacks were part of a group. The group is called al-Qaeda. It was based in Afghanistan. The US military invaded Afghanistan after these attacks. Green Berets were deployed to the country. They climbed mountains. They fought in the snow. Staff Sergeant Ronald Shurer II was in Afghanistan at this time. He was a medic in the Green Berets.

He treated wounded soldiers. He was involved in a battle in the mountains. The battle lasted six hours. There were 200 enemy fighters. Shurer remembers a 2,000-pound (907-kg) bomb that a US plane dropped. He says, "The skies were black, the sound was deafening."[5]

THE MEDAL OF HONOR

Staff Sergeant Ronald Shurer II received a special award in 2019. This award is called the Medal of Honor. It is given to troops who show bravery. It is the highest award given to a military service member. Shurer was given this award for his service in Afghanistan. He helped save many members of his team.

In 2018, SOF troops had an important mission in Afghanistan. Some ISIS fighters were in Afghanistan. Their base was in the village of Gargari. SOF members attacked this base. They arrived by helicopter. The battle lasted several days. US forces killed 167 ISIS fighters. They were able to capture the base. Josh Thiel was a lieutenant colonel. He led an SOF group in the fight. He explained the importance of this mission. He said, "ISIS was using this [base] as a site to prepare . . . high-profile attacks."[6]

SOFs may need to fly across the globe for missions on short notice.

SOF troops have also responded to terrorist attacks in other parts of the world. On April 21, 2019, a series of attacks happened in Sri Lanka. Sri Lanka is an island nation off the coast of India. ISIS terrorists detonated bombs in churches and hotels. The bombs killed more than 300 people. The US ambassador requested help. A US Army SOF team arrived in Sri Lanka less than twenty-four hours later.

GLOSSARY

altitudes

heights above the ground

contract

a signed agreement

deployed

moved into a place where missions will happen

elite

the very best

hostages

people who are held prisoner by an enemy during a war

rucksack

a bag carrying gear and supplies

terrorist

a person who carries out attacks designed to cause fear

vaccines

medicines that help prevent people from getting certain diseases

SOURCE NOTES

CHAPTER ONE: HOW DO PEOPLE JOIN THE SPECIAL OPERATIONS FORCES?

1. Quoted in Mark Price, "Unconventional Warfare Training Being Staged in 21 North Carolina Counties, Army Says," *Charlotte Observer*, August 22, 2019. www.charlotteobserver.com.

2. Quoted in Jim Garamone, "Thomas Passes Special Operations Command Reins to Clarke," *US Department of Defense*, March 29, 2019. www.defense.gov.

CHAPTER TWO: WHAT TYPES OF JOBS ARE AVAILABLE?

3. Quoted in Ryan Conroy, "Finding the Way: Special Tactics Chief Awarded Silver Star," *US Air Force*, December 18, 2017. www.af.mil.

CHAPTER THREE: WHAT IS DAILY LIFE LIKE?

4. Quoted in Diana Stancy Correll, "How the 'Horse Soldiers' Helped Liberate Afghanistan from the Taliban 18 Years Ago," *Military Times*, October 18, 2019. www.militarytimes.com.

CHAPTER FOUR: WHAT IS DEPLOYMENT LIKE?

5. Quoted in Dan Lamothe, "'What Can I Do?': Special Forces Soldier Who Fought to Save His Team in Afghanistan Receives Medal of Honor," *Washington Post*, October 31, 2019. www.washingtonpost.com.

6. Quoted in James Mackenzie, "US, Afghan Forces Clear Islamic State from Eastern District," *Reuters*, July 8, 2018. www.reuters.com.

FOR FURTHER RESEARCH

BOOKS

Roberta Baxter, *Work in the Military*. San Diego, CA: ReferencePoint Press, 2020.

Peter Kohl, *My Dad Is in the Army*. New York: PowerKids Press, 2016.

Lee Slater, *Delta Force*. Minneapolis, MN: Abdo Publishing, 2016.

Lee Slater, *Pararescue Jumpers*. Minneapolis, MN: Abdo Publishing, 2016.

INTERNET SOURCES

"Army Special Forces: Mission and History," *Military.com*, n.d. www.military.com.

"Navy SEAL Careers," *US Navy*, n.d. www.navy.com.

Joe Pappalardo, "The Air Force Is Changing How Special Ops Fighters Are Trained," *Popular Mechanics*, February 12, 2019. www.popularmechanics.com.

WEBSITES

Air Force Special Operations Command
www.afsoc.af.mil

The website of the Air Force Special Operations Command features information about air force special operations, the latest news, and photos.

Marine Forces Special Operations Command
www.marsoc.marines.mil

The website of the Marine Forces Special Operations Command has historical information, news about these special forces, and details about the leadership.

US Army Special Forces
www.goarmy.com/special-forces.html

The US Army's special forces website has information about history, training, and missions.

INDEX

Afghanistan, 34, 56, 64–65, 69–71
Air Commandos, 13, 52, 54, 65–66
Air Force Special Reconnaissance (SR), 37–39
Air Force Special Tactics, 13, 34–35
al-Baghdadi, Abu Bakr, 7–11
al-Qaeda, 69
Armed Services Vocational Aptitude Battery (ASVAB) test, 16–17, 19
Army Rangers, 12, 27, 28

breaching, 51

combat, 31–32, 34–35, 40, 47, 63
Combat Diver Qualification Course (CDQC), 53

Delta Force, 7–8, 11–12, 27
disaster relief, 5, 66–67
dogs, 4, 8, 11, 40, 41

field tests, 25–27

Green Berets, 12, 22, 26, 32, 41–44, 56, 69

Islamic State in Iraq and Syria (ISIS), 65, 67, 71, 73

Marine Raiders, 13, 41, 50
military bases, 58–60, 62

Military Entrance Processing Station (MEPS), 16
military occupational specialty (MOS), 19

Navy Sea, Air, and Land (SEALs), 13, 22, 27, 28, 37, 39–40, 48, 51, 65

Operational Detachment Alphas (ODAs), 32

parachutes, 5, 24, 26, 39–40, 43, 48, 53–55, 56, 65

rucksacks, 24, 39, 50

security clearances, 23
September 11, 2001, 68
support jobs, 41, 44–45
survival training, 24, 52

Taliban, 36, 56, 58
teamwork, 28, 50
terrorists, 7, 36, 65–69, 72–73

IMAGE CREDITS

Cover: K. Kassens/US Army/DVIDS
5: Jason Johnston/US Army/DVIDS
7: Staff Sgt. Justin Moeller, 5th SFG(A) Public Affairs/US Army/DVIDS
9: Lance Cpl. Angela Wilcox/US Marine Corps/DVIDS
10: Staff. Sgt. Daniel Snider/US Air Force/DVIDS
12: © Red Line Editorial
15: Capt. Jeremy Grant/US Army/DVIDS
18: Alun Thomas, USAREC Public Affairs/US Army/DVIDS
21: Lance Cpl. Samuel C. Fletcher/US Marine Corps/DVIDS
25: K. Kassens/US Army/DVIDS
26: K. Kassens/US Army/DVIDS
31: Staff Sgt. Iman Broady-Chin/5th Special Forces Public Affairs Office/DVIDS
33: K. Kassens/US Army/DVIDS
35: Senior Airman Dylan Gentile/US Air Force/DVIDS
38: Mass Communication Specialist 1st Class Eric Chan/US Navy/DVIDS
42: Sgt. Anthony Bryant/US Army/DVIDS
45: Sgt. Steven Lewis/US Army/DVIDS
46: Capt. Jessica Tait/US Air Force/DVIDS
49: Mass Communication Specialist 2nd Class Russell Rhodes Jr./US Navy/DVIDS
52: Sgt. Scott A. Achtemeier/US Marine Corps/DVIDS
57: Lance Cpl. William Chockey/US Army/DVIDS
59: Spc. Justin W. Stafford/US Army/DVIDS
61: Petty Officer 2nd Class Timothy M. Black/US Navy/DVIDS
63: Sgt. Jaerett Engeseth/US Army/DVIDS
64: Staff Sgt. Elizabeth Pena/US Army/DVIDS
66: Sgt. Garret Smith/US Army/DVIDS
68: Sgt. Jaerett Engeseth/US Army/DVIDS
72: Staff Sgt. Benjamin Sutton/US Air Force/DVIDS

ABOUT THE AUTHOR

Laura Platas Scott is a Cuban American writer of fiction and nonfiction. She lives in Greenville, South Carolina, with her husband and their two dogs. Her husband is a US Navy veteran.